Brown Bread and Butter

Seventy songs, rhymes and games for children, collected by Alison McMorland

Illustrated by Margaret Chamberlain

Ward Lock Educational

ISBN 0 7062 4196 7

First published 1982

Designed by Heather Sherratt

Text set in Plantin
by Sunrise Setting, Torquay, Devon
Music set by Halstan & Company Ltd, Amersham, Bucks
Printed by Nene Litho
for Ward Lock Educational
47 Marylebone Lane, London W1M 6AX
A Ling Kee Company

Contents

Acknowledgments

Many children and people have contributed to this collection, but in particular I should like to thank the following for permission to include these items:

'I have a little tiny house', 'Last night as I lay sleeping', 'Pretty pussy purr' and 'Two small dogs' translated from the Welsh by Mari Griffiths; 'I went to visit my friends one day', 'My Jenny shall have a new bonnet', and 'Sing us another one do' from Mrs J. Wheatley; 'Mama, will you buy me a' and 'My Aunt Jane' from Susanna Steele; to Mrs E. Rutherford for access to her private collection of *Camp Fire Songs*, including 'Elephants', 'My old banjo', 'Mister Wing', 'We're all together again', 'Camp fires burning', 'Come sing a round with me', 'Oom-pa-pa' and 'My mother gave me as she was able'; 'Poor old horse' from Angela Tuckett; 'Ten little witch-cats' words by E.A. Ellice-Jones, tune traditional; 'Hush my dear, the galloping men' from P. Elmhirst; 'Come butter come' from Pat Richards and 'An Austrian went yodelling' from P. Langham; 'Good morning lords and ladies' and 'On Christmas Day' from Fred Hammer's collection recorded on *Garners Gay* E.F.D.S. LP 1006; 'Where are you going to, my little pig?' and 'Billy he mounted a butterfly's back' melody lines by Bob Cort from the BBC record no. LP 12FRD 110191 *Listen with Mother*; 'The Carol of Christ's Donkey' published in *Chime Child* by Ruth Tongue (Routledge and Kegan Paul); 'Cob-o'coalin'' published in *Lancashire Songs* by H. Boardman (Oak Publications); 'My father had a horse' adapted from R. Dunstan's *Cornish Dialect and Folk Songs*; 'Jack Jintle' from ms. of A. Gilchrist housed at Vaughan Williams Memorial Library and to thank the librarians for their assistance.

Foreword

Childhood demands its own songs, from the baby and toddler being sung lullabies and nursery rhymes to children playing and singing their own games. One only has to witness these or the roaring out of songs on coach trips or around camp fires to realise the energy and life that generates from these shared experiences. For children have a great sense of occasion and this collection of songs and games reflects just that.

Collected mainly from children and people remembering the songs of their own childhood – whether by the fireside, out at play, riding in a car, celebrating Summer and Winter, or by a camp fire – there is a song for every occasion.

Introduction

Singing is the most accessible and natural form of music. Every one of us carries an inbuilt instrument, the voice, and providing there is confidence and the wish to sing everyone can. The responsibility of the teacher or parent is to provide songs that both nourish and stimulate and the larger the repertoire the better he or she is able to do so.

Many of the songs in this collection rely on spontaneity, to be sung and enjoyed before moving on, and many lend themselves to improvisation of words and actions. It is good to match one song against another, creating different moods, so that singing together becomes a way of creating an emotional as well as a musical experience.

All of these songs can be sung unaccompanied or accompanied by piano or guitar. The guitar chords are given above the stave and in some cases the use of a capo is indicated at the beginning of the song. Only one chord, the F chord, requires the use of the barre-bon and it is possible to use the first three fingers on the 2nd, 3rd and 4th frets of the 1st, 2nd and 3rd strings. The chords used are all of the simple, open-string variety and are illustrated below. They are well worth learning in order to accompany many of the songs.

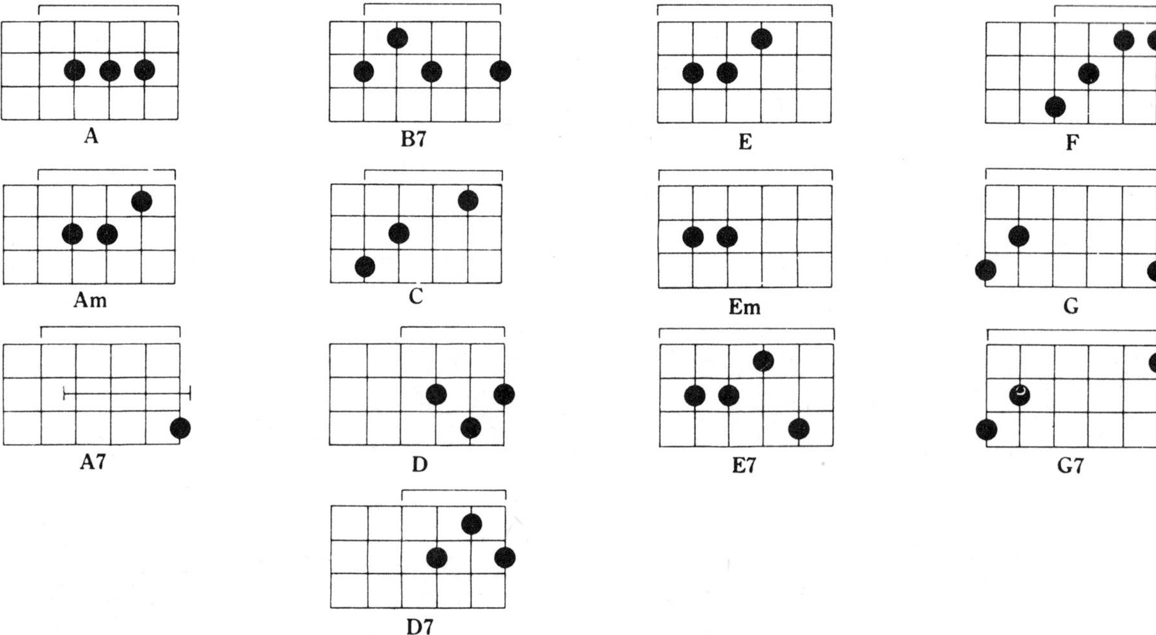

1 I have a little tiny house

I have a little tiny house,
A tiny house, a tiny house;
I have a little tiny house
That's right beside the seaside.

Chorus
Hi-dee-ho, de-hidey-hidey-ho,
That's right beside the seaside.

I do no work, I sit and watch,
And sit and watch, and sit and watch;
I do no work, I sit and watch
The high tide and the low tide.

Chorus
Hi-dee-ho, de-hidey-hidey-ho,
The high tide and the low tide.

And here I live and eat and sleep,
And eat and sleep, and eat and sleep;
And here I live and eat and sleep
Contented by the fireside.

Chorus
Hi-dee-ho, de-hidey-hidey-ho,
Contented by the fireside.

2 There was an old woman who lived in a shoe

There was an old woman who lived in a shoe
She had so many children she didn't know what to do.
She gave them some butter without any bread,
She whipped them all soundly and sent them to bed.
Sent them to bed, sent them to bed,
She whipped them all soundly and sent them to bed.

Then all those poor children crept under the clothes,
The cold pinched their fingers and also their toes,
And eating their butter without any bread,
Was not very nice for supper, they said.
Supper they said, supper they said,
Was not very nice for supper, they said.

And then the old woman who lived in the shoe,
She felt so very sorry she didn't know what to do,
She ran to the baker's to get them some bread,
And kissed them all sweetly and then they were fed.
Then they were fed, then they were fed,
She kissed them all sweetly and then they were fed.

E A B7 E
whipped them all sound - ly and sent them to bed.
B7 E
Sent them to bed, sent them to bed, She
A B7 E
whipped them all sound - ly and sent them to bed.

3 There was a tailor had a mouse

There was a tailor had a mouse,
Hi-diddle-um-cum-feedle,
They lived together in one big house,
Hi-diddle-um-cum-feedle.

Chorus
Hi-diddle-um-cum-tarum, tantum,
Through the town of Ramsey,
Hi-diddle-um-cum over the lea,
Hi-diddle-um-cum-feedle.

Now the tailor thought that the mouse was ill,
Hi-diddle-um-cum-feedle,
He gave him part of a big blue pill,
Hi-diddle-um-cum-feedle.

Chorus

Now the tailor thought his mouse would die,
Hi-diddle-um-cum-feedle,
He baked him in an apple pie,
Hi-diddle-um-cum-feedle.

Chorus

Now the pie was cut, the mouse ran out,
Hi-diddle-um-cum-feedle,
The tailor followed him all about,
Hi-diddle-um-cum-feedle.

Chorus

The tailor found that his mouse was dead,
Hi-diddle-um-cum-feedle,
So he caught another one in his stead,
Hi-diddle-um-cum-feedle.

Chorus

4 Pretty pussy purr

Pretty pussy purr,
Where did you lose your fur?
On the way to Fishguard
And the wind was bitter, sir.

Tell me, pussy sweet,
What did you have to eat?
Halibut and custard
And it was a real treat.

Listen, pussy dear,
You mustn't stray from here,
But I enjoy my journeys —
I'm a cat that knows no fear.

5 Pussy cat, pussy cat

Pussy cat, pussy cat,
Where have you been?
I've been up to London
To look at the Queen.

Pussy cat, pussy cat,
What did you there?
I frightened a little mouse,
Under her chair.

What did she give you?
Some milk in the pan.
What did you say?
Well thank you, ma'am.

B7 D7
E G
B7 D7
E7 G7
fright - ened a lit - tle mouse un - der her chair.
A C
What did she give you? Some milk in the pan.
E7 G7
A C
What did you say? Well thank you, ma'am.

6 Two small dogs

Two small dogs came walking by,
Each one wearing collar and tie;
Two small dogs in brand new suits
And each one wore four wellington boots.
Two small dogs.

Two small dogs came back again,
Through the puddles in the rain;
Each small dog had one wet foot
For each had lost one wellington boot.
Two small dogs.

Steadily

E B7
Two small dogs came walk - ing by, Each one

E
wear - ing col - lar and tie; Two small dogs in

B7
brand new suits And each one wore four

E B7 E
well - ing - ton boots._____ Two small dogs.

7 The north wind doth blow

The north wind doth blow
And we shall have snow,
And what will the robin do then, poor thing?
He'll sit in a barn
To keep himself warm,
And hide his head under his wing, poor thing.

The north wind doth blow
And we shall have snow,
And what will the swallow do then, poor thing?
Oh do you not know,
He's gone long ago
To a country where he will find Spring, poor thing.

The north wind doth blow
And we shall have snow,
And what will the dormouse do then, poor thing?
He'll curl up in a ball
In his nest snug and small;
He'll sleep till warm weather comes in, poor thing.

8 Thumbs in the thumb place

Thumbs in the thumb place, fingers all together;
This is the song we sing in mitten weather.
When it is cold it doesn't matter whether
Mittens are wool or made of finest leather.
This is the song we sing in mitten weather,
Thumbs in the thumb place, fingers all together.

Steadily

D G D
Thumbs in the thumb place, fin - gers all to - geth - er;

A7 D G A D
This is the song we sing in mit - ten wea - ther.

A7 D A
When it is cold it does - n't mat - ter wheth - er

D A7 D A7
Mit - tens are wool or made of fin - est lea - ther.

D G D
This is the song we sing in mit - ten wea - ther,

A7 D G A7 D
Thumbs in the thumb place, fin - gers all to - geth - er.

9 Three blue pigeons

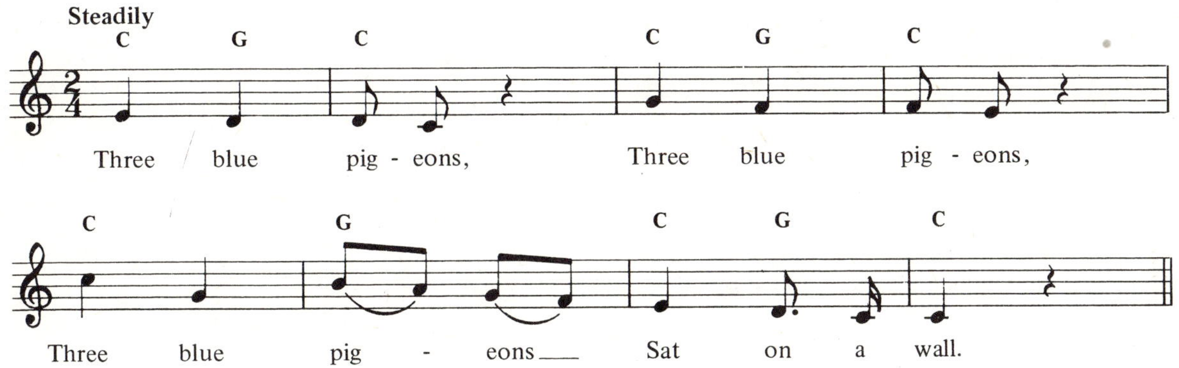

Three blue pigeons,
Three blue pigeons,
Three blue pigeons
Sat on a wall.

One flew away – (spoken)

Two blue pigeons,
Two blue pigeons,
Two blue pigeons
Sat on a wall.

One flew away – (spoken)

One blue pigeon,
One blue pigeon,
One blue pigeon
Sat on a wall.

One flew away – (spoken)

No blue pigeons,
No blue pigeons,
No blue pigeons
Sat on a wall.

One's come back – (spoken)

One blue pigeon ...

Three Blue Pigeons and Jack Jintle

Hold up three fingers of the right hand. The left hand makes the action of a bird flying away and flying back again.

10 Jack Jintle

My name is Jack Jintle,
The eldest but one,
And I can play nick-nock
Upon my own thumb.

Chorus
With my nick-nock and padlock
and sing a fine song,
And all the fine ladies come dancing along.

My name is Jack Jintle,
The eldest but two,
And I can play nick-nock
Upon my own shoe.

Chorus

My name is Jack Jintle,
The eldest but three,
And I can play nick-nock
Upon my own knee.

Chorus

My name is Jack Jintle,
The eldest but four,
And I can play nick-nock
Upon my own door.

Chorus

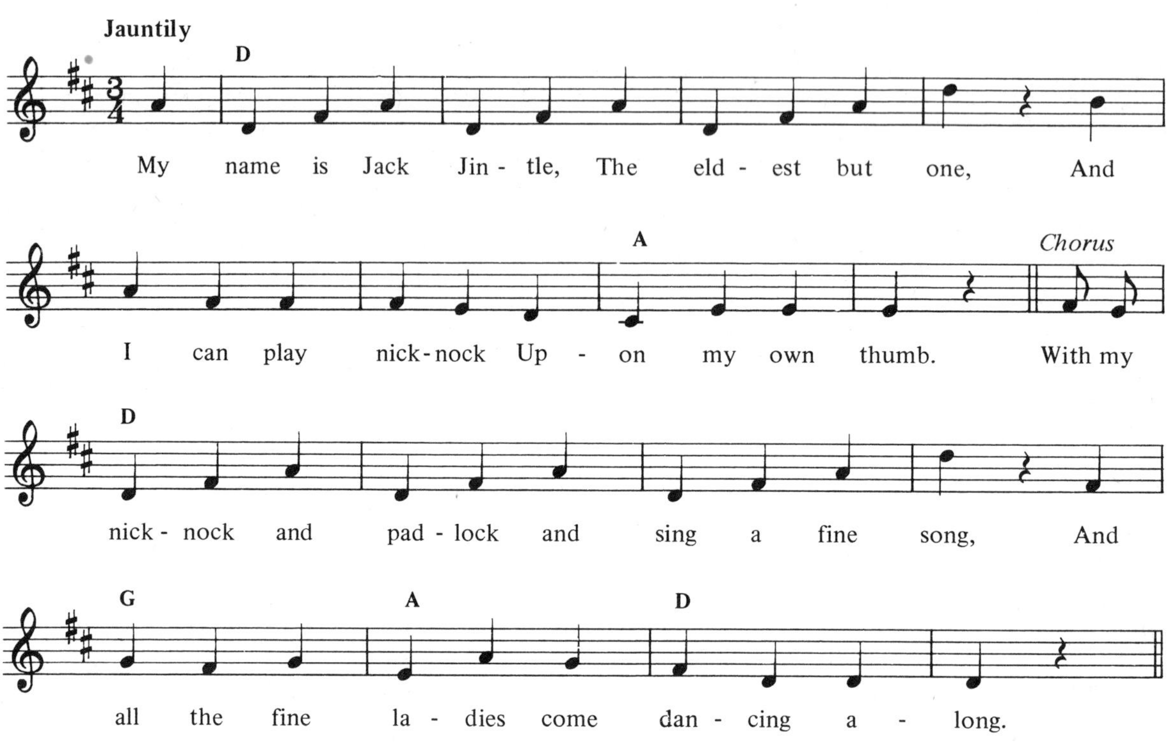

Make up actions and other verses up to ten.

11 See-saw Saccaradown

See-saw Saccaradown,
Which is the way to London Town?
See-saw Saccaradown,
Which is the way to London Town?
One foot up, the other foot down,
This is the way to London Town.
See-saw Saccaradown,
This is the way to London Town.

See-saw Jack in the hedge,
Which is the way to London Bridge?
See-saw Jack in the hedge,
Which is the way to London Bridge?
Put on your shoes and away you trudge,
This is the way to London Bridge,
Put on your shoes and away you trudge,
This is the way to London Bridge.

12 My Jenny shall have a new bonnet

My Jenny shall have a new bonnet,
My Jenny shall go to the fair,
My Jenny shall have a blue ribbon,
To tie up her bonny brown hair.

So why may I not love my Jenny?
And why may not Jenny love me?
And why may I not love my Jenny,
As well as another body?

And here is a leg for a stocking,
And here is a boot for a shoe,
And here is a kiss for a daddy,
And two for a mammy, I know.

So why must I not love my Jenny?
And why may not Jenny love me?
And why may I not love my Jenny,
As well as another body?

Guitar: capo 1st fret

Tenderly

E B7

My Jen - ny shall have a new bon - net, My

E A E B7

Jen - ny shall go to the fair, And Jen - ny shall have a blue

E B7 E

rib - bon, To tie up her bon - ny brown hair.

13 Billy he mounted a butterfly's back

Billy he mounted a butterfly's back,
  Heppity-leppity-lea.
And he flew to the top of a new-made haystack,
  With a high dumble-dumble-derry,
  High dumble-derry.

Ho-ho! said a crow that he found sitting there,
  Heppity-leppity-lea.
Don't disturb me, I beg, for no place can I spare,
  With a high dumble-dumble-derry,
  High dumble-derry.

So away they both flew till at length they did perch,
  Heppity-leppity-lea.
On the top of the steeple of Chichester church,
  With a high dumble-dumble-derry,
  High dumble-derry.

A dozen old jackdaws came pounced round their ears,
  Heppity-leppity-lea.
And bid them depart for the steeple was theirs,
  With a high dumble-dumble-derry,
  High dumble-derry.

Billy thought it was hard to be so turned away,
  Heppity-leppity-lea.
Vowed that in spite of them all he would stay,
  With a high dumble-dumble-derry,
  High dumble-derry.

14 Where are you going to, my little pig?

Where are you going to, my little pig?
I'm leaving my mother, I'm growing too big.
So big, young pig, so young, so big,
What, leaving your mother, you foolish young pig.

Where are you going to, my little pig?
I've got a new spade and I'm going to dig.
To dig, little pig, a little pig dig,
Well I never saw a pig with a spade that could dig.

Where are you going to, my little pig?
I'm going to have a nice ride in a gig.
In a gig, little pig, what, a pig in a gig,
Well I never yet saw a pig in a gig.

Where are you going to, my little pig?
I'm going to the barber's to buy me a wig.
A wig, little pig, a pig in a wig,
Why, whoever before saw a pig in a wig?

Where are you going to, my little pig?
I'm going to the ball to dance a fine jig.
A jig, little pig, a pig in a jig,
Well I never before saw a pig dance a jig,
And I never before saw a pig in a wig,
I never yet saw a pig in a gig,
I never saw a pig with a spade that could dig,
What, leaving your mother, you foolish young pig.

E A B7 E

nev - er be - fore saw a pig in a wig,__ I nev - er yet saw a

A B7 E A B7

pig in a gig,__ I nev-er saw a pig with a spade that could dig, What,

E A B7 E

leav - ing your moth - er, you fool - ish young pig.

15 My father had a horse

My father had a horse
And me mother had a mare,
My brother had a dog
And me sister had a hare.
So 'twas a ride on the horse
And a jog from the mare,
Sporting with the dog
When a-chasing of the hare.

My father had an ox
And me mother had a cow,
My brother had a pig
And me sister had a sow.
We had beef from the ox
And milk from the cow
And bacon from the pig
And more from the sow.

My father had a rooster
And me mother had a hen
My brother had a robin
And me sister had a wren.
The rooster he did crow,
We had eggs from the hen;
A song from the robin
And another from the wren.

16 Last night as I lay sleeping

Last night as I lay sleeping,
I dreamed that I was sailing
To the Isle of Man
in a frying pan,
And back again by morning.

Last night as I lay sleeping,
I dreamed that I was flying
To the Isle of Wight
on a big red kite,
And back again by morning.

Last night as I lay sleeping,
I dreamed that I was floating
To the Isle of Skye
on an apple pie,
And back again by morning.

17 Hush my dear, the galloping men

Hush my dear, the galloping men
Ride thro' the bracken and back again.
Mummy will watch her sleeping hen,
So close your eyes, my dearie.

Close your eyes and cry no more,
Mummy has told you that before.
Daddy's asleep in the big rocking chair,
So close your eyes, my dearie.

Will you be still, my fidgety, fidgety,
Fidgety, fidgety, fidgety bairn.
Will you be still, my fidgety, fidgety,
Fidgety, fidety, fidgety bairn.

Hush my dear, the galloping men
Ride thro' the bracken and back again.
Mummy will watch her sleeping hen,
So close your eyes, my dearie.

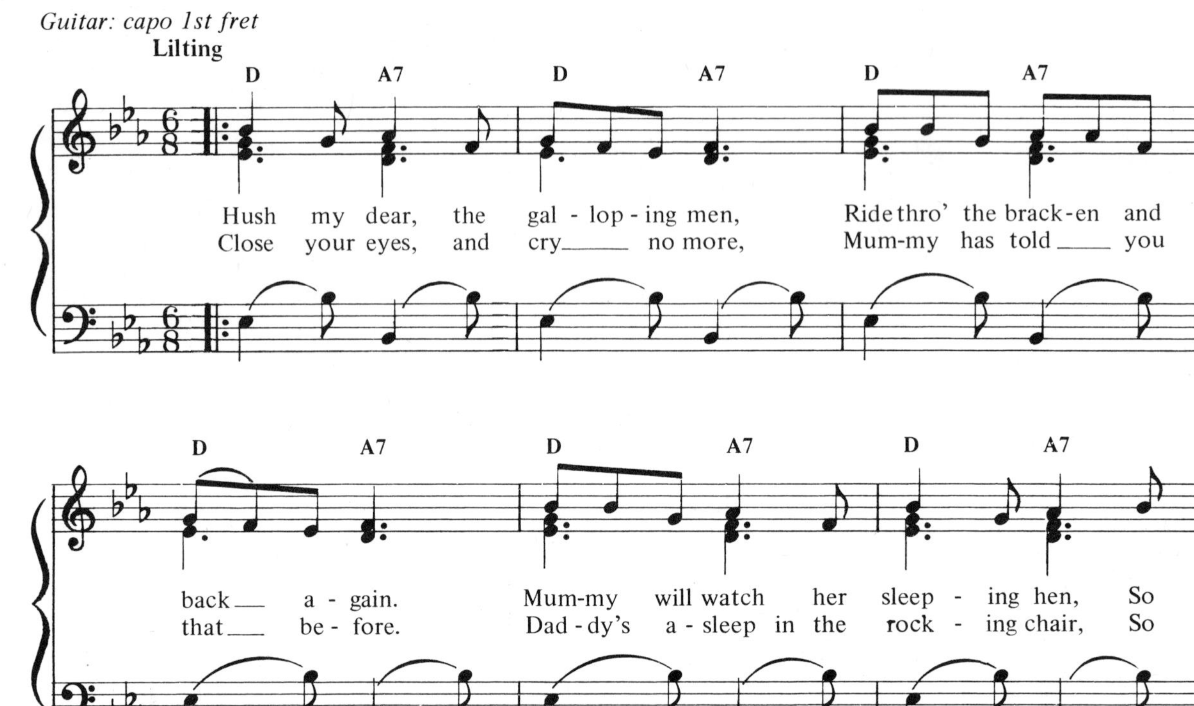

Imagine cradling a baby in your arms and softly singing it to sleep. It starts to fidget and you become just a little bit exasperated. It settles down and again you try to sing it to sleep; again it starts to fidget. This lullaby can go on and on, with the verses quietening down to a whisper and the baby is asleep.

Very fast
D A7 D D
close your eyes, my dear - ie.
close your eyes, my dear - ie.
Will you be still, my
A D
fidg - et - y, fidg - et - y, Fidg - et - y, fidg - et - y, fidg - et - y bairn.

18 I went to visit my friends one day

I went to visit my friends one day,
They only lived across the way,
They said they couldn't come out to play
Because it was their washing day.
And this is the way they washed away,
And this is the way they washed away,
And this is the way they washed away,
Because it was their washing day.

On the fifth line, do the actions of washing clothes.

Repeat verse, adding different activities, e.g. digging, sewing etc.

Last verse
I went to visit my friends one day,
They only lived across the way,
They said they could come out to play
Because it was a holiday.
And this is the way we played all day,
And this is the way we played all day,
And this is the way we played all day
Because it was our holiday.

Skip, jump or do other actions which suggest being on holiday.

19 Early in the morning

Guitar: capo 3rd fret

Moderately

A D A

Ear - ly in the morn - ing at eight o' - clock

D A E7 A

You can hear the post - man's knock.

D A

Up jumps (–) to op - en the door,

D A E7 A

One let - ter, two let - ters, three let - ters, four.

Early in the morning at eight o'clock
You can hear the postman's knock.
Up jumps (—— ——) to open the door,
One letter, two letters, three letters, four.

20 Brown bread and butter O

Brown bread and butter O,
On a summer's morning O,
If you want someone to sing,
Call on (——) (——) O.

(J) is for (Johnny) O,
On a summer's morning O,
If you want someone to sing,
Call on (——) (——) O.

The children circle round singing, with one child in the middle, who chooses someone from the ring on the fourth line.

The named child joins the one in the centre and, holding hands, they walk around forming a small circle while everyone sings his name and initial, e.g. J is for Johnny. On the eighth line 'Johnny' names someone else.

The game progresses with the named child always choosing the next child to join the circle. Gradually the inner circle grows until the outer circle has diminished to a single person. This child goes into the centre of the now large inner ring and the game starts again.

Alternatively, sing as a song with everyone having to match an adjective to their name, e.g. Jumping Johnny O.

21 Rig-a-jig-jig

Moderately

D A D

As I was walk - ing down the street, Down the street, down the street, Some-

A D

bo - dy there I chanced to meet, Hi - ho! hi - ho! hi - ho!

Faster

D A D

Rig - a-jig - jig and a - way we go, a - way we go, a - way we go;

A D

Rig - a- jig - jig and a - way we go, Hi - ho! hi - ho! hi - ho!

As I was walking down the street,
Down the street, down the street;
Somebody there I chanced to meet,
Hi-ho! hi-ho! hi-ho!

Rig-a-jig-jig and away we go,
Away we go, away we go,
Rig-a-jig-jig and away we go,
Hi-ho! hi-ho! hi-ho!

Children walk freely around until the end of the third line, when they join hands with the person nearest them. On the second verse, sung faster, they skip in rhythm to their singing.

22 Jenny Jones

We've come to see poor Jenny Jones, Jenny Jones,
Jenny Jones,
We've come to see poor Jenny Jones, how is she
today?

Oh Jenny, she is washing, washing, washing,
Oh Jenny, she is washing, you can't see her
today.

We've come to see poor Jenny Jones, Jenny Jones,
Jenny Jones,
We've come to see poor Jenny Jones, how is she
today?

Oh Jenny, she is ironing, ironing, ironing,
Oh Jenny, she is ironing, you can't see her
today.

We've come to see poor Jenny Jones, Jenny Jones,
Jenny Jones,
We've come to see poor Jenny Jones, how is she
today?

Oh Jenny, she is ill, ill, ill,
Oh Jenny, she is ill, you can't see her today.

We've come to see poor Jenny Jones, Jenny Jones,
Jenny Jones,
We've come to see poor Jenny Jones, how is she
today?

Oh Jenny, she is dead, dead, dead,
Oh Jenny, she is dead, you can't see her today.

It's red for the soldiers
And blue for the sailors
And black for the mourners
Of poor Jenny Jones.

The ghost is coming!

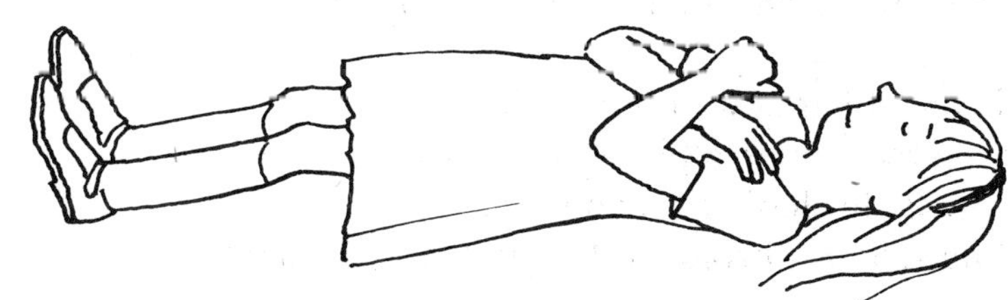

A line of children holding hands dance up to the 'mother' while singing the first verse. The mother stands in front of 'Jenny Jones', answering the questions while 'Jenny' re-enacts washing and ironing.

She rests her head in her hands for 'ill', and lies down with her eyes closed and arms crossed over her chest for 'dead'.

The children make a circle around her while singing the last verse.

Jenny jumps up, shouting 'The ghost is coming!' and chases the children until she has caught two who become the new 'Jenny Jones' and 'mother' to begin the game again.

23 Elephants

One elephant went balancing
Step by step on a piece of string.
He thought it was such an amusing stunt,
He called for another little elephant.

Two elephants went balancing
Step by step on a piece of string.
They thought it was such an amusing stunt,
They called for another little elephant.

Continue adding another elephant until:

Ten elephants went balancing
Step by step on a piece of string.
One little elephant made a rush,
The string it broke and they all went crash!

Shape right arm into an elephant's trunk and 'balance' carefully on an imaginary line, walking along it in a swaying movement. Choose another elephant by 'touching' with trunk, who then follows after the leader, repeating the choosing of another 'elephant'. Gradually a long line forms which crashes to the floor at the tenth 'elephant'.

24 Teddy bear, teddy bear

Teddy bear, teddy bear, touch the ground,
Teddy bear, teddy bear, turn around,
Teddy bear, teddy bear, go down the street,
Teddy bear, teddy bear, wash your feet.
Teddy bear, teddy bear, go up the stairs,
Teddy bear, teddy bear, say your prayers.
Teddy bear, teddy bear, switch off the light,
Teddy bear, teddy bear, say goodnight.

25 Ring-a-ring-a-rosies

Ring-a-ring-a-rosies,
A pocket full of posies,
Atishoo! Atishoo!
We all fall down.

Penny on the water, (spoken)
Penny on the sea,
Up jumps the little fish
And up jumps me!

(Jump up and start the game again.)

Two simple ring games with the children skipping around and falling to the ground on the fourth line.

26 The leaves are green

The leaves are green, the nuts are brown,
They hang so high, they won't come down.
Leave them alone till frosty weather,
Then they will all come down together.

27 One little bluebird

One little bluebird in my window,
One little bluebird in the sky,
One little bluebird in my window,
I-tiddily-i-tie-tie.

Take a little step and dance in the corner,
Take a little step and dance on the floor,
Take a little step and dance in my window,
I-tiddily-i-tie-tie.

Stand in a circle with raised arms to make arches. One person on the outside of the ring is the 'bluebird' who weaves in and out of the arches during the first verse. On the second verse the 'bluebird' stands behind another person and taps on his shoulder – that person now becomes a bluebird also. Both weave in and out, repeating the sequence until only one arch remains.

28 O a-hunting we will go

O a-hunting we will go,
A-hunting we will go,
We'll catch a fox and put him in a box
And never let him go.

O a-hunting we will go,
A-hunting we will go,
We'll catch a fish and put him in a dish
And never let him go.

O a-hunting we will go,
A-hunting we will go,
We'll catch a whale and put him in a pail
And never let him go.

O a-hunting we will go,
A-hunting we will go,
We'll catch a rat and feed him to the cat
And never let him go.

With a partner the children make a long line (about six to eight couples is best). The top two hold hands and skip down the aisle and back again to the first two lines while the rest clap. They separate, turn and skip down the outside of the line, the other children following. At the bottom of the line they make an archway and the children duck under it, joining hands as they do so. The new top couple start the game again.

29 I am a little Dutch girl

I am a little Dutch girl, little Dutch girl, little Dutch girl,
I am a little Dutch girl from Holland, you see.

I am a little Dutch boy, little Dutch boy, little Dutch boy,
I am a little Dutch boy from Holland, you see.

And now I do not like you …

And why don't you like me? …

Because you stole my necklace …

And here is your necklace …

And now I do not like you …

And why don't you like me?…

Because you stole my dolly …

Then here is your dolly …

And now we're getting married …

And now we've got a baby …

And now we've got a windmill …

Essentially a duet that can be acted freely to interpret the words in pairs or a group.

30 There came a girl from France

Guitar: capo 1st fret

Briskly

There came a girl from France,
There came a girl from Spain,
There came a girl from the U.S.A.
And this is how they came.

Hopping on one foot,
Hopping on one foot,
Hopping, hopping, never stopping,
Hopping on one foot.

Jumping up and down,
Jumping up and down,
Jumping, jumping, never bumping,
Jumping up and down.

Turning round and round,
Turning round and round,
Turning, turning, never burning,
Turning round and round.

They decided to go home,
They decided to go home,
Hopping, jumping, turning, skipping,
They all skipped home the same.

These skipping rhymes can be used for action songs or for plain singing as well as for skipping to.

31 Do you want a cigarette Sir?

Do you want a cigarette Sir?
No Sir,
Why Sir?
Because I've got a cold Sir.
Where did you get the cold Sir?
Up the North Pole Sir.
What were you doing there Sir?
Catching Polar bears Sir.
How many did you catch Sir?
One Sir, two Sir, three Sir, four Sir.
What happened to the fifth Sir?
It caught me Sir.

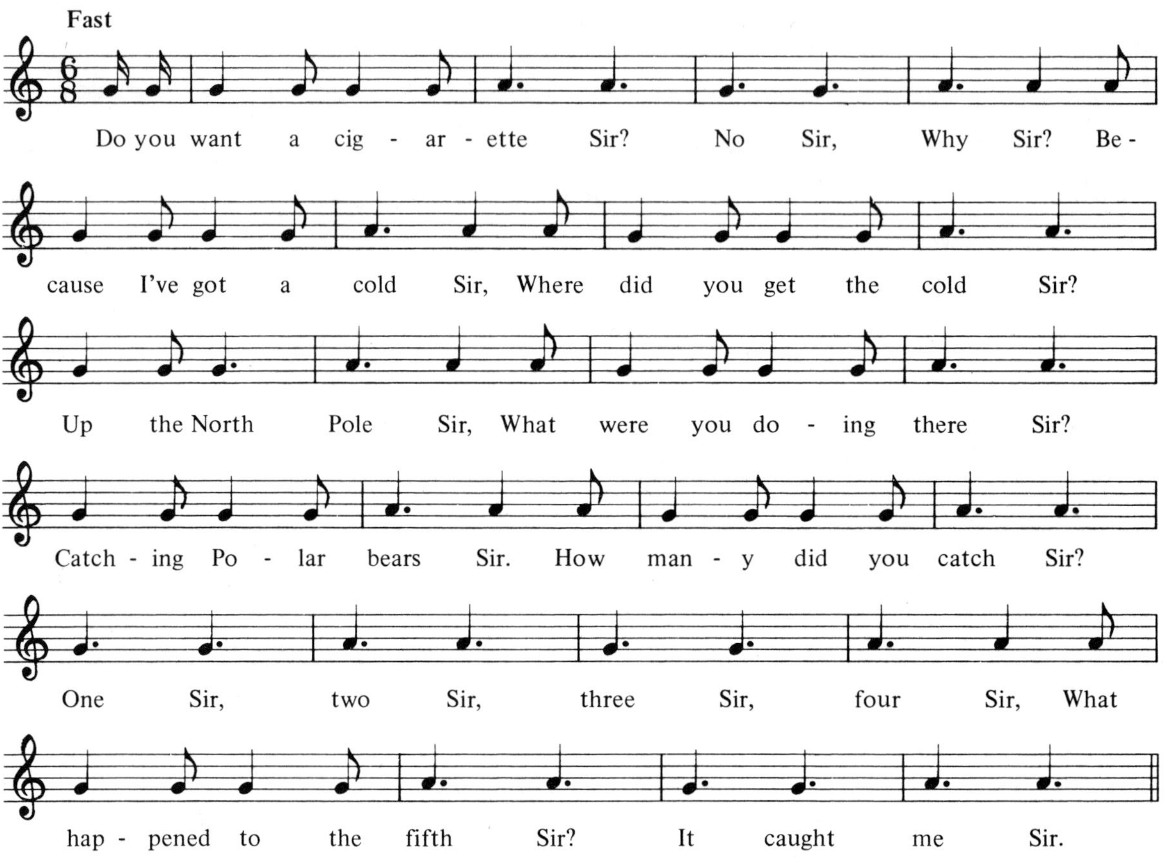

Put a ball in an old stocking, stand against a wall and bounce it from left to right of the body in rhythm to the music, or use it for skipping to.

32 Bluebells, cockle shells

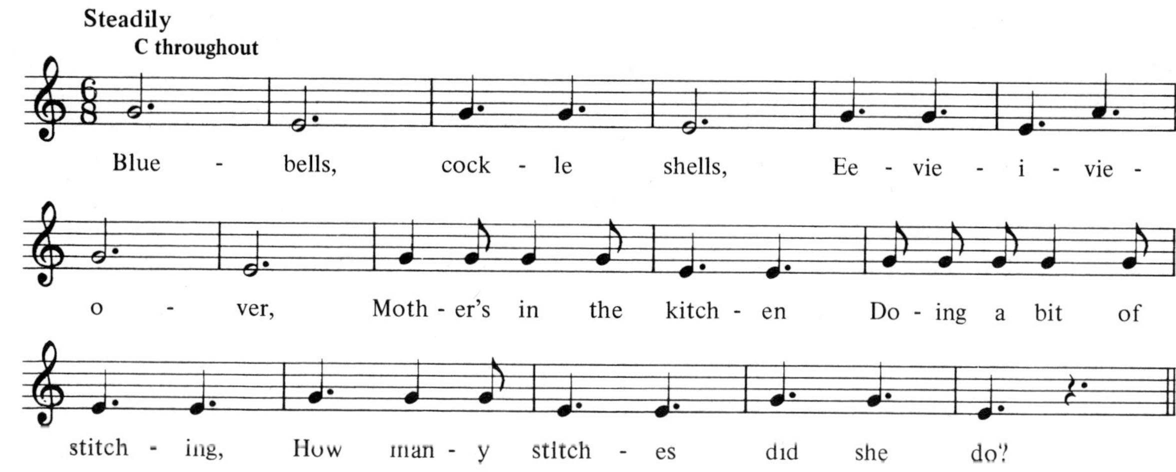

Bluebells, cockle shells,
Eevie-ivie-over.
Mother's in the kitchen
Doing a bit of stitching.
How many stitches did she do?

One, two, three …

33 Jelly on the plate

Jelly on the plate,
Jelly on the plate,
Wibble wobble, wibble wobble,
Jelly on the plate.

Custard on the floor,
Custard on the floor,
Pick it up, pick it up,
Custard on the floor.

Sausage in the pan,
Sausage in the pan,
Turn it over, turn it over,
Sausage in the pan.

Biscuits in the tin,
Biscuits in the tin,
Eat them up, eat them up,
Biscuits in the tin.

Fire on the floor,
Fire on the floor,
Put it out, put it out,
Fire on the floor.

34 My Aunt Jane

My Aunt Jane, she pulled me in,
She gave me tea out of her wee tin,
Half a bap with sugar on the top,
Three black lumps out of her wee shop.

My Aunt Jane, she's awful smart,
She bakes wee rings and an apple tart,
And when Hallowe'en comes round,
Beside that tart I'm always found.

My Aunt Jane has a bell at the door,
A wide step stone and a clean swept floor,
Candy apples and hard green pears,
Conversation lozenges.

My Aunt Jane can dance a jig,
And sing a ballad round a sweetie pig,
Wee red eyes and a cord for a tail,
Hanging by a farthing nail.

My Aunt Jane has a great wee shop,
With lucky bags and lime juice rock,
Cinnamon buds and yellow man,
And brandy balls in a bright tin can.

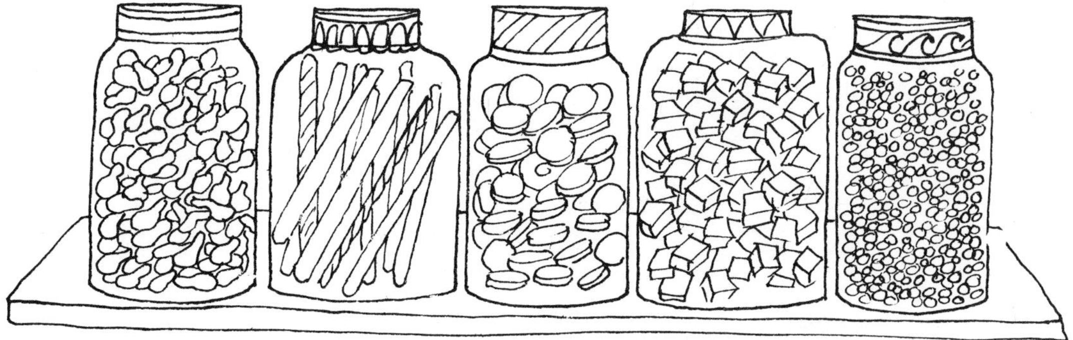

35 Shrove Tuesday, Shrove Tuesday

Shrove Tuesday, Shrove Tuesday
When Jack went to school,
His mother made pancakes
And she left them to cool.

She roast them, she toast them,
She made them so hot,
She put too much pepper on them
And she poisoned poor Jack.

36 All around the maypole

All around the maypole merrily we go,
Hip-a-chip-a-cherry, singing as we go,
All the happy pastimes around the village green,
Sporting in the sunshine,
Hoorah, hoorah, hoorah, May Queen.

Oh I'm a lily, don't you see,
Just come from the meadows green,
And if you wait a little while,
I will dance you the maypole style.

Hail to this month, this merry month of May,
Hail to the trees and flowers,
Hail to this month, this merry month of May,
As we go to show our bowers.

A A E
Queen. Oh I'm__ a lil - y,__ don't you
A E A
see, Just come from__ the mea - dows green, And
D
if you wait a lit - tle while,
E A
I will dance you the May - pole style,

Since early times the coming of Spring has been celebrated through song and dance, probably originating in the pagan belief that the singing of May songs would dispel the gloom of Winter, and within living memory Lancashire children have had their own May Queen celebrations. They would decorate either a short, hand-held pole, or crossed hoops, with paper rosettes, ribbons and bells. A May Queen would be chosen amongst themselves, and dressed in white with an old lace curtain for a train. The Queen and her followers would progress around the streets collecting money that would later buy lemonade and biscuits.

37 Buttercups and daisies

Buttercups and daisies,
Pretty coloured flowers,
Growing in the sunshine,
Floating with the showers.

One stalk through another,
Till they catch and hold,
Join a chain of silver
To a chain of gold.

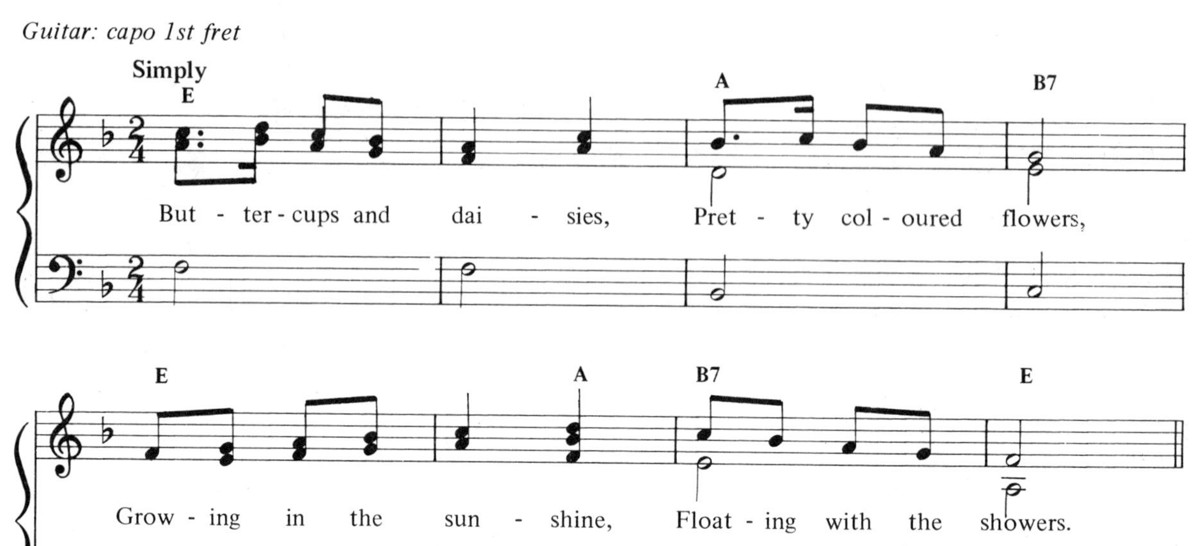

38 Good morning lords and ladies

Good morning lords and ladies,
It is the first of May.
We hope you'll view our garland,
It is so bright and gay.

Chorus
For it is the first of May,
For it is the first of May,
Remember, lords and ladies,
It is the first of May.

We gathered them this morning,
All in the early dew,
And now we bring their beauty
And fragrance all for you.

Chorus

The cuckoo comes in April,
It sings its song in May,
In June it changes tune,
In July it flies away.

Chorus

And now you've seen our garland,
We must be on our way,
So remember lords and ladies,
It is the first of May.

Chorus

The making of freshly-gathered flowers into a garland, which was then taken from door to door by children, accompanied the custom of May Carolling in many country areas. This May song comes from the Northamptonshire border.

39 A branch of may

A branch of may, it does look gay,
But before your door it stands.
It is but a sprout, but it's well spread about,
By the work of our poor hands.

I have a bag upon my arm,
It is drawn with a silken string.
It only wants a few more pence,
To line it well within.

Arise, arise, my pretty fair maid,
And take our may bush in.
For if it is gone before morning comes
You'll say we have never been.

Come give us a cup of your sweet cream,
Or a jug of your brown beer.
And if we live to tarry in the town,
We'll call another year.

40 Hop tune-ay

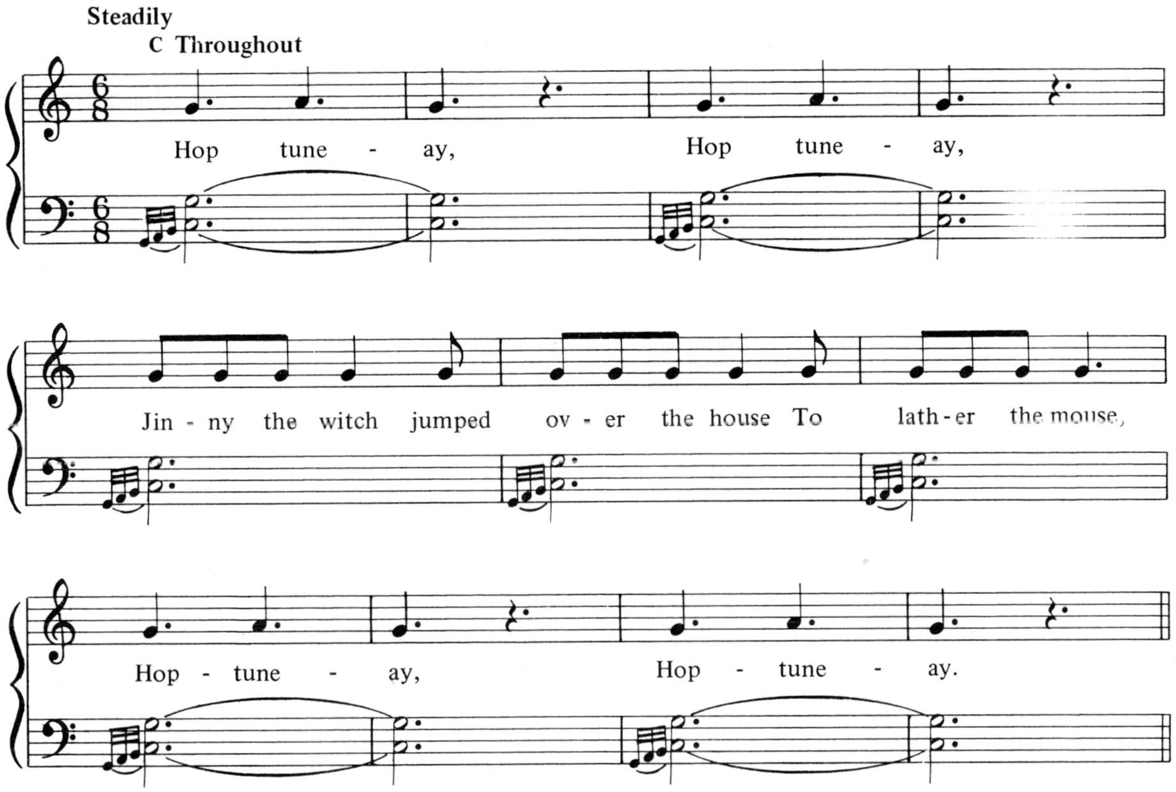

Steadily
C Throughout

Hop tune - ay, Hop tune - ay,

Jin - ny the witch jumped ov - er the house To lath - er the mouse,

Hop - tune - ay, Hop - tune - ay.

Hop tune-ay, hop tune-ay
Jinny the witch jumped over the house
To lather the mouse,
Hop tune-ay, hop tune-ay

41 Cob-o'-coalin'

Chorus
We come a cob o'coalin', cob o' coalin', cob o'coalin',
We come a cob o'coalin' for bonfire neet.

The first to come in is a collier you see,
With his pick and his shovel all ready to dig.
He digs it and picks it and then it does fall,
And that is the way that we gather cob coal.

Chorus

And the next to come in is a sailor you see,
With a bunch of blue ribbon tied under his knee,
He's travelled through England and France and through Spain,
And now he's returned to owd England again.

Chorus

The last to come in is a miser you see,
He's a hump on his back and he's blind of an e'e,
He's a weary owd fella and he wears a pigtail,
And all his delight is in drinking strong ale.

Chorus

Now down in yon cellar there's an owd umbrella,
There's nowt on you cornish but an owd pepper
 pot,
Pepper pot, pepper pot, mornin' till neet,
If you give us nowt we'll pinch nowt an' bid you
 goodneet.

Chorus

And down in yon cellar there's plenty of bugs,
They've eaten mi stockin's an' part of mi clogs,
I'll get a sharp knife an' we'll cut their yeds off,
An' we'll have a good supper of bugs' yeds and
 broth.

Spoken
Up a ladder and down a wall,
Tuppence or threepence will please us all.

At one time around Hallowe'en great fire festivals took place all over England. Lancashire in particular had many ceremonial fires and at the beginning of this century children still gathered fuel for the bonfires to burn on the hills around. Often disguised, they went in bands from door to door wishing good luck.

To this day, children in the Oldham area sing a shortened version of this song and collect money for fireworks.

42 Witches' coil

The tallest child is decided upon and everyone gets into a long line holding hands.

The last child begins to lead the line in a circle around the tallest, creating a winding motion and chanting quietly for two or three times:

Wind up the bush faggot,
Wind it tight,
Wind it by day and
Wind it by night!

As the circle becomes tighter the volume increases, changing to:

Stir up the dumplings
The pot boils over.

And as the winding reaches a conclusion the voices should reach a pitch as they jump up and down on the last chant. Immediately start to unwind again starting quietly and getting louder saying:

Round and round the old oak tree
I love the boys and the boys love me.

until everyone flops down exhausted.

43 Hag-a-leena, mag-a-leena

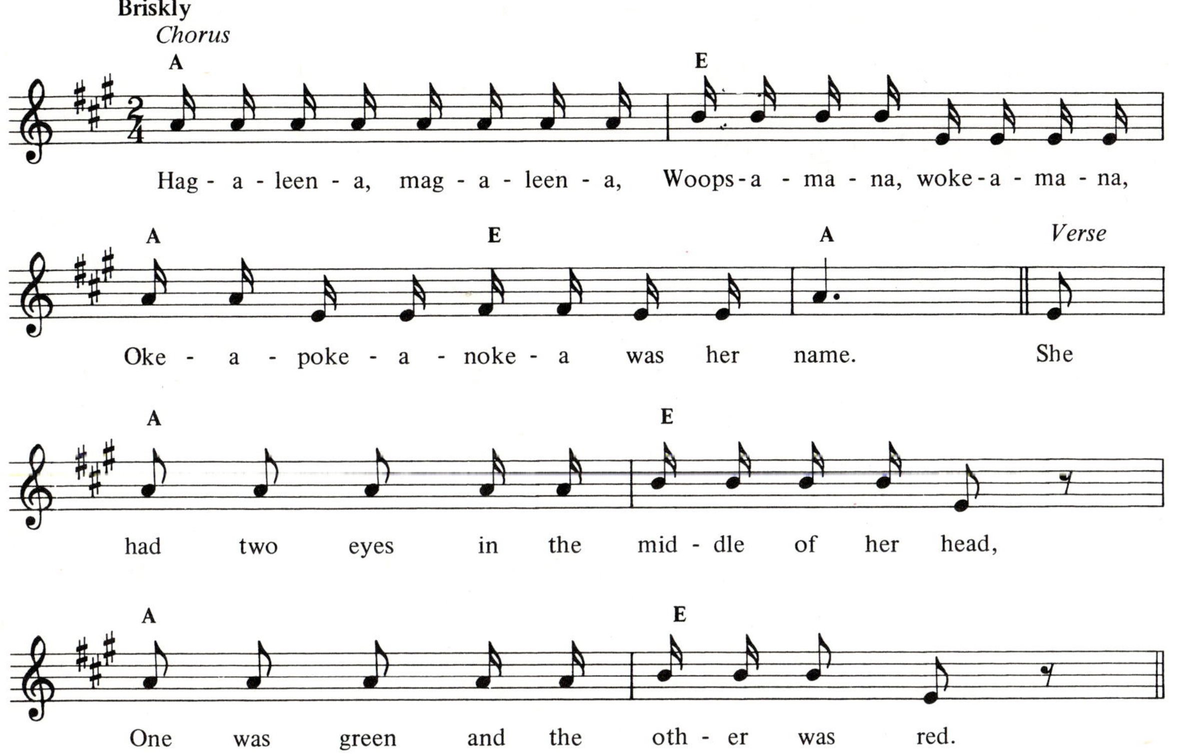

Chorus
Hag-a-leena, mag-a-leena,
Woops-a-man-a, woke-a-man-a,
Oke-a-poke-a-noke-a was her name.

She had two eyes in the middle of her head,
One was green and the other was red.

Chorus

She had two hairs in the middle of her head,
One was alive and the other was dead.

Chorus

She had two teeth in the middle of her mouth,
One pointed north and the other pointed south.

Chorus

She had two toes in the middle of her feet,
One was bone and the other was meat.

Chorus

44 Ten little witch-cats

Ten little witch-cats walking in a line,
One stopped to wash himself,
So then there were nine.

Nine little witch-cats staying out so late,
One fell fast asleep,
So then there were eight.

Eight little witch-cats flying up to Heaven,
One landed on the moon,
So then there were seven.

Seven little witch-cats playing witching tricks,
One said the wrong spell,
So then there were six.

Six little witch-cats stealing honey from a hive,
One was chased by a bee,
So then there were five.

Moderately

G D G

Ten lit - tle witch - cats walk - ing in a line,

D7 G A7 D

One stopped to wash him-self, So then__ there were nine.

G D G

Nine lit - tle witch - cats stay - ing out so late,

D7 G C D7 G

One fell fast a - sleep, So then there were eight.

Five little witch-cats sitting at a cottage door,
One was called inside,
So then there were four.

Four little witch-cats wondering what to be,
One became a prize cat,
So then there were three.

Three little witch-cats walking round the zoo,
One was frightened by a big fish,
So then there were two.

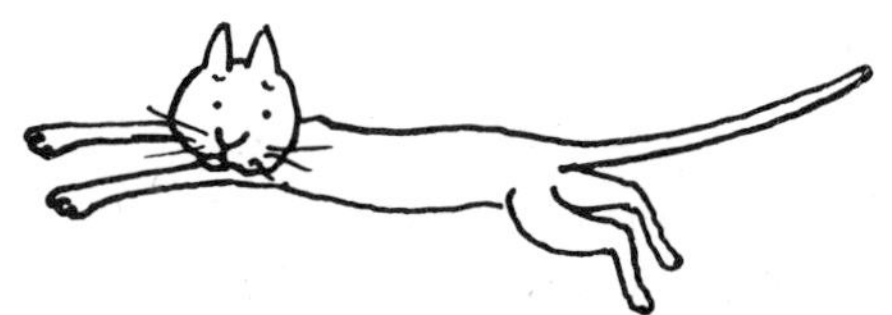

Two little witch-cats going for a run,
One met a lady cat,
So then there was one.

One little witch-cat missing all the others,
Wished a magic wish,
And back came all his brothers.

45 The carol of Christ's donkey

I gave Him my manger all full of sweet hay,
I knelt with the shepherds on Chrissimas Day.
The Star it shone over and loud did I bray,
Gloria in excelsis! Christ the Lord is born!

I carried Him softly on Egypt's dark road,
King Herod was angered to find we had gone,
His soldiers had stayed us afore, had he known.
Jubilate! Amen! Christ the Lord is free!

I carried Him proudly on Palm Sun-en-day,
On leaves of the Tree I did walk all the way.
The people rejoiced, they did carol and say,
Hosanna in the Highest! Christ the Lord is King!

They lifted Him down from the cruel Cross-tree,
And sadly I bore Him to Gethsemane.
My tears fell so fast that I hardly could see.
Miserere Domine! Christ the Lord is dead and gone!

Our Lord He is risen! He walks by the sea,
A Cross on my back for the world for to see.
Now blest be all Donkeys! Now blessed be He!
Alleluia! Alleluia! Christ the Lord is King of Heaven!

Within the folk memory the donkey has special significance throughout the life of Jesus. Its power of speech, shedding of tears and cross on its back are supposedly proof of its holiness.

46 On Christmas day it happened so

On Christmas Day it happened so,
Down in those meadows for to plough;
As he was ploughing all on some land,
Up came Sweet Jesus Himself at last.

Oh man, oh man, what makes thou plough,
So hard upon the Lord's birthday?
The farmer answered him with great speed,
For to plough this day I have got need.

His wife and children out at play,
His beast and cattle are almost lost.
His beast and cattle they died away,
For ploughing on our Lord's birthday.

47 St Day Carol

Now the holly she bears a berry as white as the milk,
And Mary she bore Jesus all wrapped up in silk.

Chorus
And Mary she bore Jesus Christ our Saviour for to be,
And the first tree that in the greenwood,
It was the holly, holly, holly,
And the first tree that in the greenwood, it was the holly.

Now the holly she bears a berry as green as the grass,
And Mary she bore Jesus who died on the cross.

Chorus

Now the holly she bears a berry as black as the coal,
And Mary she bore Jesus who died for us all.

Chorus

Now the holly she bears a berry as blood it is red,
And Mary she bore Jesus who rose from the dead.

Chorus

In the week before Christmas, the people and brass band of St Day's, Cornwall, gather in the square to sing carols. This one is always sung and is known as the St Day Carol (after the Breton Saint) because it was first recorded in this village.

48 Poor old horse

When I was young and in my prime
And in my stable lay,
They gave to me the very best corn
And eke the choicest hay.
Poor old horse, poor old mare.

Now I am old and past my prime
And good for nothing more;
I am not worth a peck of corn
Nor scarce a wisp of straw.
Poor old horse, poor old mare.

My master used to ride me out
O'er many a hedge and stile,
O'er many a fence and ditch I've gone
And borne him many a mile.
Poor old horse, poor old mare.

Now I am old and past my prime
And good for nought at all,
I'm forced to eat the sour grass
Beside the churchyard wall.
Poor old horse, poor old mare.

My hide I'll to the huntsman give,
My shoes I'll throw away,
The dogs shall eat my rotten flesh
And that's how I'll decay.
Poor old horse, poor old mare.

In Nottinghamshire and Derbyshire a mummers' play and song called 'The Old Horse' was performed at Christmas. A player held the skull of a horse painted black and red and supported on a wooden fore-leg. A man, covered with a cloth to represent the body of the horse, snapped its formidable jaws from the inside (M.H. Mason *Nursery Rhymes and Country Songs* 1878). As with all mummers' plays the theme is of death and resurrection – the rebirth of nature.

49 We're off in a motor car

We're off, we're off, we're off in a motor car,
Sixty coppers are after us
And we don't know where we are.
We're going around the corner eating apple pie,
One of the coppers said give us a bit,
So we sloshed it in his eye!

50 Mama, will you buy me a ?

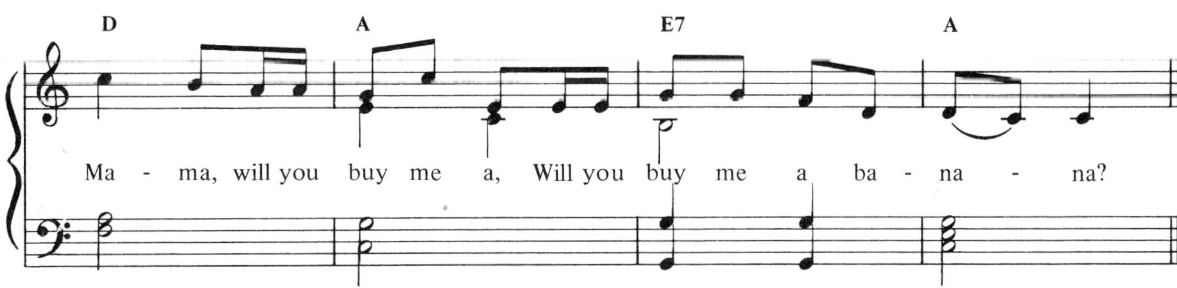

Mama, will you buy me a,
Will you buy me a,
Will you buy me a,
Mama, will you buy me a,
Will you buy me a banana?

Mama, will you peel the skin,
Will you peel the skin,
Will you peel the skin,
Mama, will you peel the skin,
The skin of my banana?

Mama, do you wanna bite,
Do you wanna bite,
Do you wanna bite,
Mama, do you wanna bite,
A bite of my banana?

Mama, you took too much,
You took too much,
You took too much,
Mama, you took too much,
Too much of my banana.

Mama, you're a greedy glut,
You're a greedy glut,
You're a greedy glut,
Mama, you're a greedy glut,
You've eaten my banana.

Mama, will you buy me a,
Will you buy me a,
Will you buy me a,
Mama, will you buy me a,
Will you buy me a banana?

51 There were ten in the bed

There were ten in the bed and the little one said,
  Roll over, roll over.
So they all rolled over and one fell out,
As he hit the floor he gave a shout,
Please remember, please remember
To tie your pyjama cords together,
Single beds are only made for one.

There were nine in the bed and the little one said,
  Roll over, roll over.
So they all rolled over and one fell out,
As he hit the floor he gave a shout,
Please remember, please remember
To tie your pyjama cords together,
Single beds are only made for one.

There were eight in the bed ...

There was one in the bed and the little one said,
  Goodnight!

Please re - mem-ber, Please re - mem-ber to
Em G D G
tie your py - ja - ma___ cords to - geth - er,
D G A D
Sin - gle beds are on - ly made for one.

52 B-A-Bay

B-A-Bay,
B-E-Bee,
B-I-Bicky-by,
B-O-Bow-bicky-by-bow,
B-U-Boo,
Bay-bicky-by-bow-boo.

D-A-Day,
D-E-Dee,
D-I-Dicky-die,
D-O-Dow-dicky-die-dow,
D-U-Doo,
Day-dicky-die-dow-doo.

Fee-A-Fay,
Fee-E-Fee,
Fee-I-Ficky-fie,
Fee-O-Foe-ficky-fie-foe,
Fee-U-Foo,
Fay-ficky-fie-foe-foo.

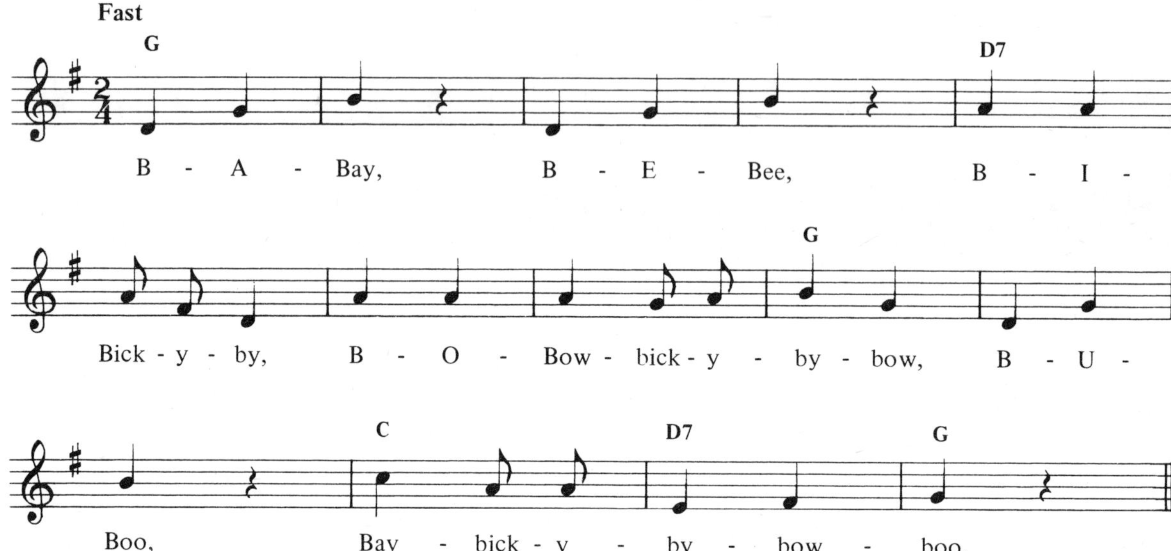

53 Mister Wing

Oh Mister Wing, we sing-a-ling-a-ling
With all our hearts for you,
We hope there'll be some thing-a-ling-a-ling
That we can do for you.
In Autumn, Winter, Spring-a-ling-a-ling
And all the whole year through,
We'll sing-a-ling-a-ling
And ring-a-ling-a-ling
And ting-a-ling-a-ling for you!

54 Three little angels

Three little angels all dressed in white
Tried to get to heaven on the end of a kite.
The kite string was broken, down they all fell,
They couldn't get to heaven, so they all went to —

Two little angels all dressed in white
Tried to get to heaven on the end of a kite.
The kite string was broken, down they all fell,
They couldn't get to heaven, so they all went to —

One little angel all dressed in white
Tried to get to heaven on the end of a kite.
The kite string was broken, down she fell,
She couldn't get to heaven, so she went to —

Three little devils all dressed in red
Tried to get to heaven on the end of the bed.
But the bedpost was broken, down they all fell,
They couldn't get to heaven, so they all went to —

Two little devils all dressed in red
Tried to get to heaven on the end of the bed.
But the bedpost was broken, down they all fell,
They couldn't get to heaven, so they all went to —

One little devil all dressed in red
Tried to get to heaven on the end of the bed.
But the bedpost was broken, down he fell,
He couldn't get to heaven, so he went to —

Don't be mistaken,
Don't be misled,
They couldn't get to heaven, so
They all went to bed.

55 My old banjo

I used to play an old banjo,
I played it on my knee.
But now the strings are broken
And it's no more use to me.

I took it to a mender's shop
To see what he could do.
He said the strings are broken
And it's no more use to you.

56 Sing us another one do

There was an old man with a beard,
Who said it is just as I feared,
Two owls and a hen,
Four larks and a wren
Have all built their nests in my beard.

Chorus
That was a cute little song,
Sing us another one do.

There was an old dame of Antigua,
Who said to her son, what a pig you are.
When we have roast mutton
You eat like a glutton,
You know it is bad for your figua.

Chorus

Moderately

G D
There was an old man with a be - ard, who said it is just as I

G C
fear - ed, Two owls and a hen, Four larks and a wren Have

D G *Chorus* G
all built their nests in my be - ard. That was a

D G
cute lit - tle song, Sing us an - oth - er one do.

There was an old man from Calcutta,
Who coated his tonsils with butter.
It converted his snore
From a thunderous roar
To a soft oleaginous mutter.

Chorus

There was an old woman of Chewa,
She was riding a bike when it threw her.
The butcher came by,
Said missis don't cry,
And he fastened her on with a skewer.

Chorus

There was a young lady of Ealing,
She walked upside down on the ceiling,
She said, O by heck,
I've a crick in my neck
And it is a peculiar feeling.

Chorus

There was a young lady from Ryde,
Who ate some green apples and died.
The apples fermented
Inside the lamented
And made cider inside her inside.

Chorus

57 We're all together again, we're here

We're all together again,
We're here, we're here;
We're all together again,
We're here, we're here,
And we don't know when
We'll be all together again,
Singing we're all together again,
We're here, we're here.

58 Camp fires burning

Camp fires burning, camp fires burning,
Draw nearer, draw nearer;
In the gloaming, in the gloaming,
Come sing and be merry.

59 Hokey Pokey

Chorus
Hail to Britannia, God save the Queen,
These times be good times or else we wouldn't sing.
Hokey Pokey penny a loafie, taste before you buy,
Singing oh what a merry place is England.

Old King Cole was a merry old soul and a merry old soul was he,
Singing oh what a merry place is England,
He called for his pipe and he called for his bowl,
Singing oh what a merry place is England.

Chorus

Jack and Jill went up the hill to fetch a pail of water,
Singing oh what a merry place is England,
Jack fell down and broke his crown and Jill came tumbling after,
Singing oh what a merry place is England.

Chorus

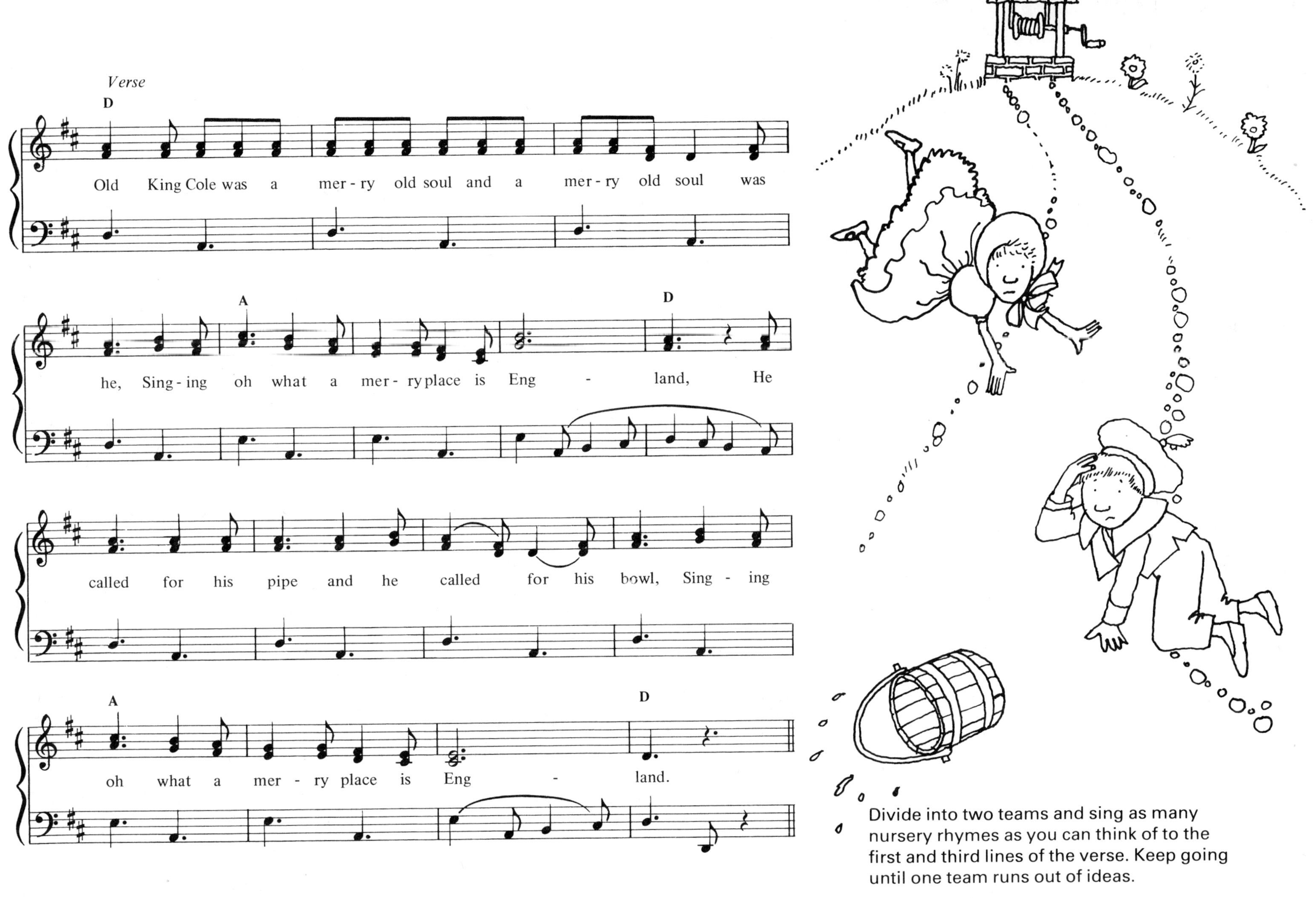

Divide into two teams and sing as many nursery rhymes as you can think of to the first and third lines of the verse. Keep going until one team runs out of ideas.

60 One ginger beer

One ginger beer,
Two ginger beer,
Three ginger beer,
Four ginger beer,
Five ginger beer,
Six ginger beer,
Seven, seven ginger beer.

O you can't put your muck in our dustbin,
Our dustbin, our dustbin;
O you can't put your muck in our dustbin,
Our dustbin's full.

Fish and chips and vinegar, vinegar, vinegar,
Fish and chips and vinegar, pepper, pepper,
pepper-pot!

These three songs are sung simultaneously by three different groups.

61 Oom-pa-pa!

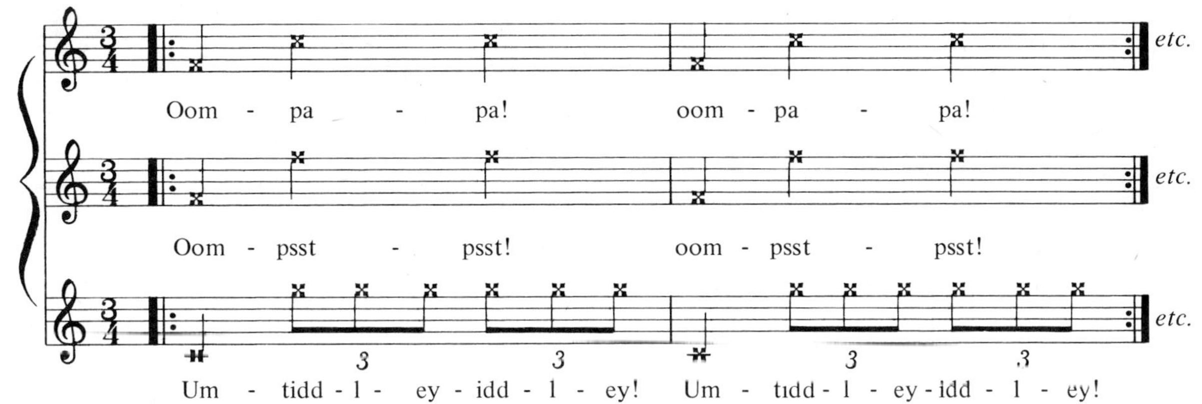

Oom-pa-pa!
Oom-pa-pa!
Oom-pa-pa!
Oom-pa-pa!

Oom-psst-psst!
Oom-psst-psst!
Oom-psst-psst!
Oom-psst-psst!

Um-tiddley widdley!
Um-tiddley-widdley!
Um-tiddley-widdley!
Um-tiddley-widdley!

These three rhythms are said simultaneously by three groups. A fourth group hums to the tune of 'O you can't put your muck in our dustbin' in a bagpipe voice! (Hold your nose and as you sing knock your throat gently with the other hand.)

62 I'm bringing home a baby bumble bee

ZZ–ZZ–ZZ–ZZ

I'm bringing home a baby bumble bee.
Won't my mummy be so pleased with me.
I'm bringing home a baby bumble bee.
OW! It's stung me!

I'm squashing up a baby bumble bee.
Won't my mummy be so pleased with me.
I'm squashing up a baby bumble bee.
Ooh! Look at that!

I'm licking up that baby bumble bee.
Won't my mummy be so pleased with me.
I'm licking up that baby bumble bee.
Oh! I feel sick!

I'm bringing up that baby bumble bee.
Won't my mummy be so pleased with me.
I'm bringing up that baby bumble bee.
Ugh! What a mess!

I'm sweeping up that baby bumble bee.
Won't my mummy be so pleased with me.
I'm sweeping up that baby bumble bee –

ZZ–ZZ–ZZ–ZZ

Oh — Oh!

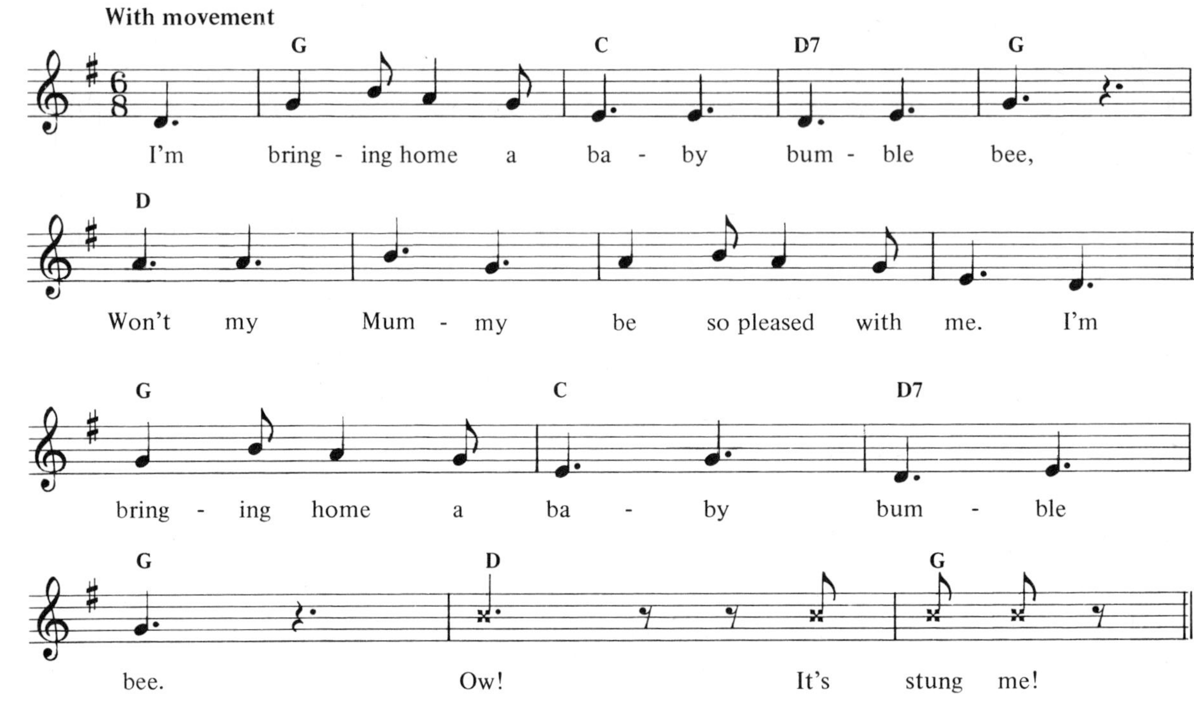

Catch imaginary bee in cupped hands.
React to being stung.
Rub hands together.
Lick hands.
Look disgusted.
Pretend to be sick.
Sweep floor.
Listen and look for the ...
... new bee sounds.
Start song again.

63 Nobody likes me

Nobody likes me, everybody hates me,
I'm going down the garden to eat worms.
Long, thin, slimy ones, short, fat, juicy ones,
Ooey, gooey, fuzzy, wuzzy worms!

Bite off their heads and suck their juice,
O how they wriggle and squirm.
Long, thin, slimy ones, short, fat, juicy ones,
Ooey, gooey, fuzzy, wuzzy worms!

The short, fat, fuzzy ones slip down easily,
The long, thin, slimy ones stick-ick!
Nobody knows how I survive
On a hundred worms a day.

64 An Austrian went yodelling

An Austrian went yodelling on a mountain so high,
When along came **an avalanche** interrupting his cry.
Oh-la-zwi–
Ol-di-ra-di-(k)hee-ah, ol-di-ra-cuckoo, SSHH!
Ol-di-ra-di-(k)hee-ah, ol-di-ra-cuckoo, SSHH!
Ol-di-ra-di-(k)hee-ah, ol-di-ra-cuckoo, SSHH!
Ol-di-ra-di-(k)hee-ah-oh.

An Austrian went yodelling on a mountain so high,
When along came **a grizzly bear** interrupting his cry.
Oh-la-zwi–
Ol-di-ra-di-(k)hee-ah, ol-di-ra-cuckoo, SSHH!
GRRR!

An Austrian went yodelling on a mountain so high,
When along came **a Bernadin** [St Bernard dog]
interrupting his cry.
Oh-la-zwi–
Ol-di-ra-di-(k)hee-ah, ol-di-ra-cuckoo, SSHH!
GRRR! WOOF! WOOF!

An Austrian went yodelling on a mountain so high,
When along came a **pretty girl** interrupting his cry.
Oh-la-zwi–
Ol-di-ra-di-(k)hee-ah, ol-di-ra-cuckoo, SSHH!
GRRR! WOOF! WOOF! KISS! KISS!

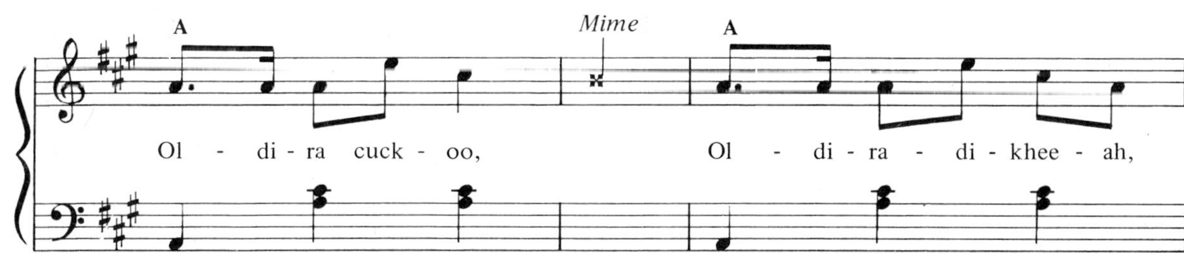

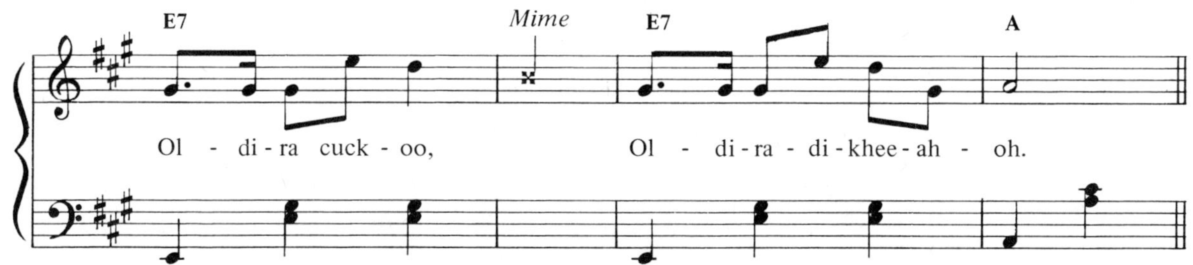

An Austrian went yodelling on a mountain so high,
When along came his **ugly wife** interrupting his cry.
Oh-la-zwi–
Ol-di-ra-di-(k)hee-ah, ol-di-ra-cuckoo, SSHH!
GRRR! WOOF! WOOF! KISS! KISS!
SCHLA! SCHLA!
Ol-di-ra-di-(k)hee-ah, ol-di-ra-cuckoo, SSHH!
GRRR! WOOF! WOOF! KISS! KISS!
SCHLA! SCHLA!
Ol-di-ra-di-(k)hee-ah, ol-di-ra-cuckoo, SSHH!
GRRR! WOOF! WOOF! KISS! KISS!
SCHLA! SCHLA!
Ol-di-ra-di-(k)hee-ah-oh.

First learn the chorus and the following actions that go with it. Slap knees quickly as you sing OH-LA-ZWEE; now slap knees – clap hands – snap finger and thumb of both hands as you sing:

OL–DI	RA-DI	(K)HEE-AH
(knees)	(clap hands)	(snap fingers)

OL–DI	RA-CUC	KOO
(knees)	(clap hands)	(snap fingers)

Repeat ending with:

OL–DI	RA-DI	(K)HEE-AH OH
(knees)	(clap hands)	(snap fingers)

Mime sliding gesture with arm.
Mime hands and paws of a dog.
Mime kissing to the left and right.
Slap imaginary face from left to right.

65 My mother gave me as she was able

My mother gave me as she was able
A bowl, a bucket, a dish and a ladle.
A bowl, a bucket, a dish and a ladle,
A bowl, mother, a bowl.

My mother gave me as she was able
Two bowls, two buckets, two dishes, two ladles.
Two bowls, two buckets, two dishes, two ladles,
Two bowls, mother, two bowls.

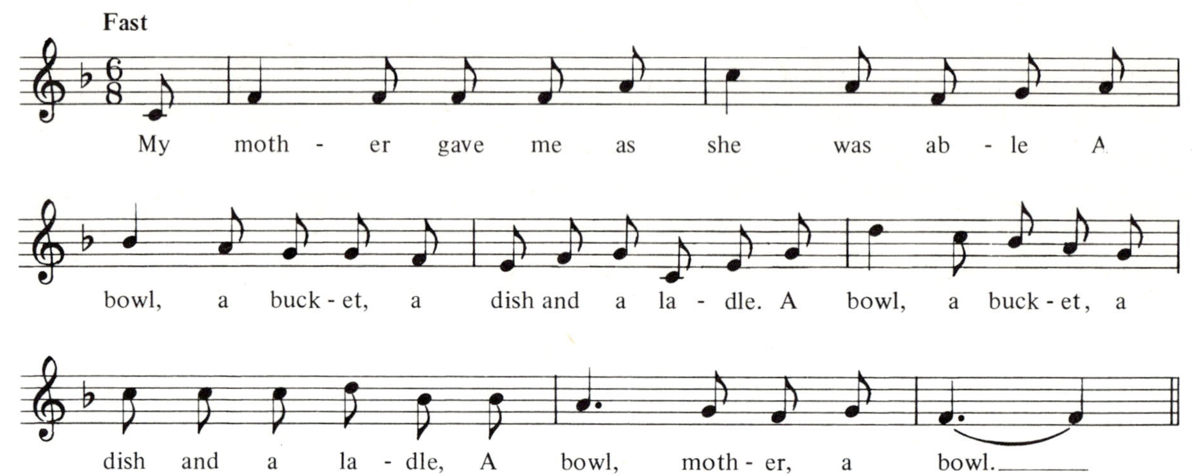

Each time the name is sung mime the shape of:

a bowl; a bucket; a dish, and a ladle.

66 Who stole the cookie?

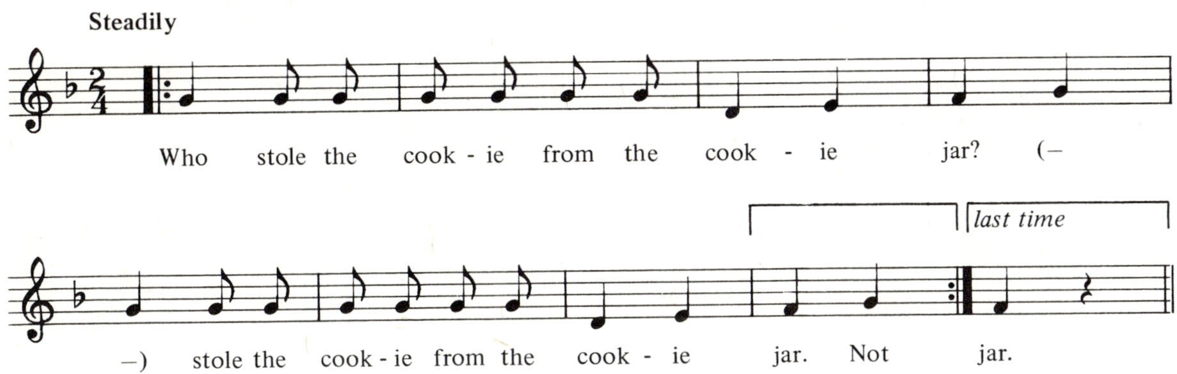

Who stole the cookie from the cookie jar?
(— —) stole the cookie from the cookie jar.
Not I stole the cookie from the cookie jar.
Then who stole the cookie from the cookie jar?
(— —) stole the cookie from the cookie jar.
Not I stole the cookie from the cookie jar.
Then who stole the cookie ...

Stand in a circle and clap first your own hands and then the hands of the person on either side of you in rhythm to the melody. Sing the first two lines, naming someone who answers on the third line and shouts out another person's name. The ring always asks the question, 'Who stole the cookie from the cookie jar?'

67 Come sing a round with me

Come sing a round with me,
Let us united be,
Then we shall all agree
To sing in pleasant harmony.

68 Come butter come

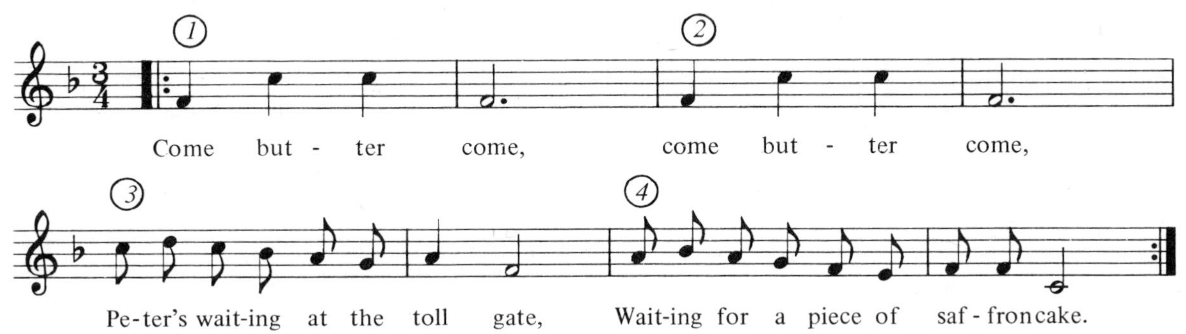

Come butter come, come butter come,
Peter's waiting at the toll gate,
Waiting for a piece of saffron cake,
Come butter come, come butter come.

69 Have you seen the ghost of John?

Have you seen the ghost of John,
Long white bones and the rest all gone;
Oooh — Oooh —
Wouldn't it be chilly with no skin on.

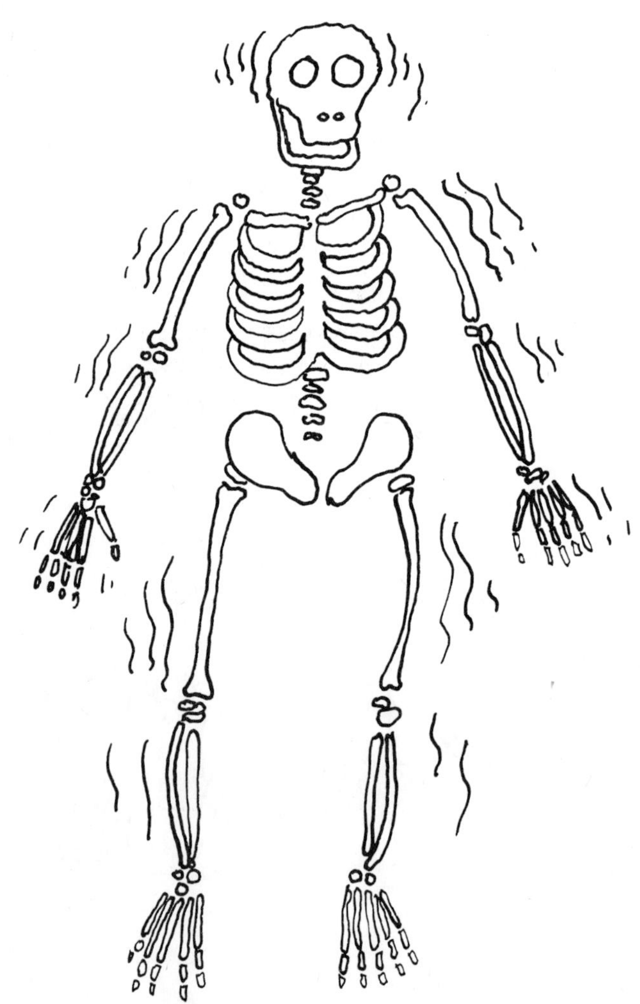

70 A woman in a churchyard sat

A woman in a churchyard sat,
Oo-oo oo-oo, ah-ah ah-ah;
Very short and very fat,
Oo-oo oo-oo, ah-ah ah-ah;
She saw some corpses carried in,
Oo-oo oo-oo, ah-ah ah-ah;
Very tall and very thin,
Oo-oo oo-oo, ah-ah ah-ah.

Woman to the corpses said,
Oo-oo oo-oo, ah-ah ah-ah;
Shall I be like you when I am dead,
Oo-oo oo-oo, ah-ah ah-ah;
Corpses to the woman said,
Oo-oo oo-oo, ah-ah ah-ah;
Yes, you'll be like us when you are dead,
Oo-oo oo-oo, ah-ah ah-ah;
Woman to the corpses said –
A A A A A G H !

Index of first lines

Song books from Ward Lock Educational

The Funny Family
Alison McMorland
An entertaining selection of singing games, nursery rhymes and folk songs, which will be enjoyed and treasured by young and old alike. Simple guitar chords and melody line or piano accompaniment are provided, and children will enjoy the humorous illustrations. Alison McMorland has collected these items through her experience as a folk singer and collector of children's games.

Knock at the Door
Jan Betts
A comprehensive collection of songs, poems and rhymes which are popular today with young children. Very simple guitar chords and melody lines are provided, while the delightful illustrations will provide many hours of enjoyment for children.

Folk Carols for Young Children
Barbara Cass-Beggs
A bright, international selection of carols and nursery rhymes, which includes many traditional Christmas carols as well as some for other festivals from several countries. A brief note on the origin of each carol and suggestions for accompanying dance movements are included.

Sing as You Grow
Brenda I. Piper
The original songs in this delightful collection have been written especially for the very young, and are designed to encourage physical, mental, emotional and social skills. Understanding and enjoyment of the simple melody lines and easily learnt words is enhanced by the clear, bright illustrations, while guitar chords are included, together with suggestions for untuned percussion.

Music titles from Ward Lock Educational

Musical Starting Points in the Classroom
Jean Gilbert
This book outlines a number of starting points in musical activities that can help the class teacher with no specialist music training to integrate the subject into the daily timetable. The singing games, finger plays and songs in the book encourage movement and dance and, ultimately, physical and emotional development. The concentration that is encouraged by these pleasurable activities will undoubtedly benefit the child's all-round learning ability.